P|

AFTEF

MW01031902

"Simple to follow, to the point, and won't overwhelm you!"
-*Natalie Rathweg*

"Excellent Resource! This is an excellent book for the formerly incarcerated and should be made available for all those returning from prison or jail."
-*Katherine Vockins*

This is the advice people need when coming home. John Mandalla has written a tremendously useful, greatly needed book about people returning from prison. This book is a much-needed resource, not only for the persons themselves, but for their friends and families.
-*Brent Buell*

A handy reference guide for anyone about to be released, recently released or anyone with a loved one recently released. Small enough to keep in your pocket or purse to quickly refer to when in a situation that you may not be familiar with when transitioning back into society.
-*LaTanya*

"We need to get this book in the hands of as many people we know who are incarcerated or are coming out of prison. There are simple, step-by-step instructions on how to prepare yourself, what goals to set, how to reach them, and how to remain inspired to create a life for yourself while maintaining peace with your situation."
-*Amazon Customer*

Thanks

The author wishes to sincerely thank those individuals who have supported this important endeavor and he expresses his sympathy to the families of victims of crime throughout the world, and to all those that have been wrongly convicted and/or executed.

Table of Contents

Here Are Some Words of Wisdom:

Peace cannot be kept by force. It can only be achieved through understanding.

-Dostoyevsky

If, at first, the idea is not absurd, then there is no hope for it.

-Einstein

When you know everything there is to know, it is then that you soon find you really don't know anything.

-A. Quatroni

The only negative force that works against a person is his own stubbornness to change, listen or adapt.

-A. Quatroni

Injustice anywhere is a threat to justice everywhere.

-Martin Luther King Jr.

The measure of a society can be gauged by the way it treats its prisoners.

-Dostoyevsky

INTRODUCTION

Over the next 5 years, more than 600,000 men and women will be released from our prisons and back into society. Of that number, current research suggests that within three years more than 50% will return to prison as a result of a violation of parole, a violation of post-release supervision, and/or because of the commission of a new crime. It is, therefore, the hope of the author that through the distribution and use of this planner, that men and women will increase their chances of successful transition back into mainstream society. This book is packed with information you will need to ease your transition back into society. Use it well.

> ***DON'T BE JUST ANOTHER STATISTIC!***
>
> ***DO SOMETHING WITH YOUR LIFE!***

AFTER PRISON: A WAY TO SUCCEED

Let's face it, the prison system is geared to help you return to it. We don't want to create controversy or be branded as being too opinionated, but it is just a big business like any other, and as long as you contribute to this business it will be waiting for you to return and perpetuate its survival.

Why not try and do something that will help you stay away from this big business? Look at this book/planner, listen to your Parole Office, do as he or she says, and stay free of and out of the system.

There are several "Prison Release Guides" out there, many of which are so overblown and full of information that you will probably never use. It is enough to make your head spin! This book, *After Prison, A Way To Succeed*, is simple to follow, to the point, and won't overwhelm you with so much information that your attention span will be taxed.

We're quite sure that if you follow the instructions set forth in this book, you'll be on your way to leading a successful, productive, and free life, without the worry that you'll be returned to prison.

> *KEEPING IT SIMPLE IS THE KEY TO EVERYTHING! IF YOU KEEP YOUR LIFE SIMPLE, THEN NOTHING CAN COMPLICATE IT!*

We are not going to give you hundreds of addresses to look into, we're not going to preach, and we're not going to baby you. We are going to point you in the right direction and then the rest is up to you.

> ***This book assumes that you have absolutely made up your mind to stay out of prison.***

You can read this book as soon as you are incarcerated, somewhere along the way, or right at the end before you are released.

We are also assuming that you have set
yourself up with a place to stay upon release.
It could be a home, shelter, or a close relative.
This book will help you get a job, get needed
documents in order, and give you a place to
store your information and release history. It
will help you pace yourself and provide a "pit
stop" at times to measure your progress in
becoming a totally free person.

NOTES:

PREFACE

> **Read this book and stay out of the system!**
>
> **Remember, every day out there, no matter how bad it might seem, is still better than the best day you might have in prison.**

Throughout the prison system in the United States, prison administration programs are struggling to prepare incarcerated men and women for release into society.

Today, it costs more than 50 billion dollars a year to house over 1 million men and women, and funding for reintegration programs are minimal, especially in light of our nation's shift from rehabilitation to one of warehousing.

Our policy gurus seem to be on a throw-away-the-key mentality, ignoring the realization that a large majority of people formerly incarcerated will someday be released.

Consequently, many individuals are less prepared to succeed upon release, because they have the stigma of a prison sentence as well as their original problem, whatever it may have been (drugs, violence, etc.).

> *THE CREATIVE SPIRIT IS THE MOST UNTAPPED SOURCE OF ENERGY IN THE UNIVERSE.*

Viable skills on par with the 21st century service society are simply not offered in the prison setting. Vocational programs either do not exist or are horrendously outdated.

In addition, higher education programs such as college, once available to prisoners, have now been eliminated since Congress elimination of Pell grants throughout the United States.

Privately funded college and work programs are working thru the Hudson Link for higher education program begun in New York some 25 years ago. The recidivism rate is less than 1% of attendees and their return home.

TO BE SUCCESSFUL
REMEMBER
TO USE EVERY PIECE OF
INFORMATION THAT YOU
COME ACROSS!

This is all part of the change from rehabilitation to the warehousing mindset. Prison will no longer be a place where a person that has committed a crime can truly repay his or her debt to society by coming out a changed and "improved" person, *unless those inmates initiate that change themselves*. Frequently, they emerge in worse condition.

Most notably, prison programs fall short in preparing men and women for their eventual release. Few prisons have valid release plans that assist in finding housing, employment, sources of varied information and most importantly, support systems. As a result of the above, most prisoners are slated to fail upon release and perpetuate the recidivist structure that is there waiting for them.

This book is not simply to read, it is meant to be *used*. There are spaces you can fill in with information you will need before or upon release. You can begin to use it *now*, so when you are released, you can continue to use it as a planner, reminder, and data source.

At the back of the book, you will find a place where you can have a potential employer place their signature and you can then account for your attempts to obtain employment. If your Parole Officer asks if you are looking for a job you can *show* him or her that you are, rather than simply having him or her take your word for it. Be responsible and consistent.

WE WILL NOT BE JUDGED BY THE PURITY OF OUR ACTIONS, BUT BY THE INTEGRITY OF OUR COMPROMISES.

-BILL WEBER

CHAPTER 1
Where, When, & How to Begin

Most prisoners believe that once they are released from prison they will begin dealing with reentry into society. This is a fallacy – Wise people will tell you that preparations for release from prison begin on the *first day of your arrest.*

> ## START PLANNING NOW

For many prisoners, Determinate Sentencing is the rule today, therefore prisoners know the exact date on which they will be released, barring any unforeseen consequences such as a disciplinary action resulting in loss of good time.

Time and time again, behavior in prison is a clear-cut insight into whether a person will be successful upon release or will soon fail. If you spend all your time watching TV and playing cards, well, then you are already on the path of returning to prison after getting out.

> ## *IT IS UP TO YOU!*

This being the case, most prisoners can plan for their release. Begin now by filling in the dates below to remind yourself, depending on the sentence you have.

> ## SET RELEASE DATE:
>
> _____
>
> ## EARLIEST POSSIBLE RELEASE DATE:
>
> _____

Six months before your earliest release date is a good time to begin preparing and using this book and planner. Here is a simple checklist for you to begin the process of preparing for your release.

You will be surprised at how many things you can mark off your list in no time at all. Moreover, it will give you a "visual hope" and confidence that you are moving in the right direction towards your successful transition into society.

> *SMART PEOPLE LEARN FROM THE MISTAKES THEY MAKE, WISE PEOPLE LEARN FROM THE MISTAKES OF OTHERS.*

NOTES:

A List of Release Needs

These are the things you should have before or upon release. Check these off as you obtain them:

____ Address Book/ Phone Number Lists
____ Birth Certificate
____ Budget Plan
____ Certificates/ Degrees
____ Credit Report
____ DD-214 Military Papers
____ Driver's License/DMV Record Review
____ Medical Records
____ Medication List
____ Parole Plan
____ Rap Sheet
____ Resource List
____ Resume
____ Short/Long-Term Goals & Plan
____ Social Security Card
____ Time Management

If your crime involved drugs or if you have a history of drug use, you should also have the following:

_____ Inpatient / Outpatient programs in your area

_____ List of nearby 12-Step meeting places

_____ Mandated Support Groups you will be attending

NOTES:

CHAPTER 2
How to Get Your Needed Documents

Address Book – Everyone should have an address and phone number book to keep their vital addresses and phone numbers handy. It can be a small memo pad or a nice leather-bound, line-paper book you might spend some money for at a stationary store. If you attend A.A. or N.A. meetings, it is good to have a book with phone numbers you can call if you are having a problem with something. Get one or use a separate piece of paper or a pad if necessary.

Birth Certificate – It is important to have a copy of your Birth Certificate. If you did not get it while incarcerated through a Transitional Services Center or equivalent, you can get it by writing to your local Department of Health.

Budget Plan – When you get a job and begin to make a paycheck or even if you already have some money saved upon release, it is a good idea to have a budget plan. Determine your costs of living for the week, which will include food, housing, transportation, clothing, and any other expense you might have for that week and add it up. Deduct that from your pay for that week, and make sure you have enough left over in case of an unforeseen circumstance, like a car breakdown that needs to be repaired. When you get settled and start making regular paychecks, make sure that your food, rent (if any), utilities (gas and electricity), and any car insurance or other critical bill is paid right off the top.

These monthly bills are going to be in your budget plan permanently, unless you move, or something changes in your monthly living expenses. Be sure that you set up a budget plan that allows you to save for these monthly payments out of your weekly or bi-weekly check and pay them first, leaving enough for food and clothing.

Certificates/ Degrees – These are important if you have gained a High School GED or a college degree while incarcerated. Also, any vocational certificates you might have earned should be kept in a safe place. These will all help towards procuring a job, and in some cases, employers will hire you based on your experience regardless of your criminal history, if you pick the right employer and are honest with them. If you have a prior degree or certificate, you will need to write to the school or college where you obtained it and request a copy.

Credit Report – In this day and age, it is vital that you obtain a credit report for yourself. There have been instances where unsuspecting people have had others use their Social Security numbers, obtained illegally, to get credit cards and buy things without paying for them. If this has happened to you, you will never know unless you get a credit report on yourself.

The three major reporting centers you can call to obtain their mail-in forms are:

EQUIFAX – 1-800-685-1111 or www.equifax.com

TRANSUNION – 1-877-322-8228 or
www.transunion.com

EXPERIAN – 1-888-397-3742 or
www.experian.com

Be alert to changes in your credit reports. Someone else may be using your Social Security number or credit card number to make purchases that you will pay for in the end!

Here's a tip: You can contact each credit reporting agency once per year, so if you spread out your requests for a credit report to one of these agencies every four months, you can always have an updated report for yourself. This will help you quickly find out about someone who might be using your credit for fraudulent purposes.

DD-214 (Military Service Records) – If you served in the military, you should have a copy of your service record. If you have not obtained one while incarcerated, you can normally go to a local recruiting center and they will give you the form to fill out. On the form, it will direct you to the address where you'll need to send the form to get the required record, since it's different if you were in the Army, Navy, Air Force, Marines, or other branches of the military.

Driver's License – Every state has a Department of Motor Vehicles (DMV). They will be able to provide you with a printed record of any unpaid tickets or suspensions on your license. To find out about your license status, write to the state Department of Motor Vehicles where you obtained that license and ask for an abstract. Once you receive the abstract, you can begin to consider what steps you need to take to clear up any outstanding tickets or determine what will need to be done to restore your license to a valid status. If you do not have a license, and never had one, you will need to go to your local DMV office to determine what types of ID you will need, and what steps you'll need to take to get a license. Upon release, most Parole Officers (P.O.) will not allow you to drive for the first 6 months, although in some cases you will be allowed to drive. Depending on your status, you will need to clear this with your P.O. before doing anything. Remember this: You can look up your local DMV in the phone book or on the web.

Medical Records - Before release – If you are taking any type of medication or have any health problems, you should request copies of your medical records. You may have to pay for the copies of your medical records but it is critical that you have these so that if you see a physician on the outside, you can give them to him or her and it will save them a lot of time on your case. To obtain records from a specific hospital you may have been treated at, you will need to get the address of that hospital and write to them.

Medication List: This goes hand in hand with getting your medical records. If you take medications, especially crucial ones like HIV meds or blood pressure meds, always make a list of them and keep it with you. If anything happens to you, doctors will be able to take steps to make sure you are not given anything that will cause an adverse reaction to other medications you may be taking.

If you are diabetic or have serious health issues, look into getting a Medic-Alert bracelet, which will make it even easier for doctors to quickly determine your needs if you are unable to communicate with them.

Parole Plan - You should have written a detailed parole plan before you were released. In some states, you must do this before being released. You should set up for yourself a daily planner, which is described in another chapter in this book that you can follow on a daily and/or monthly basis. Without a plan, you are basically lost when you are released. Make one now!

Rap Sheet - You should always get a copy of your rap sheet, particularly if you have more than one arrest. Frequently, arrests are entered into your rap sheet that did not result in a conviction. In some instances, you may be able to have those issues fixed. For example, if your arrest was "sealed in favor of the accused," that arrest will only be shown to certain agencies requesting your rap sheet. If you find a mistake on your rap sheet, a form is included so that you can challenge an entry. You may also have another state's or federal rap sheet. If so, you will need to write to the state's Department of Criminal Justice Services, and to the federal one as well. These addresses differ from state to state, and (unfortunately) cannot all be included here. However, you get the idea.

For a Federal Rap Sheet, write to:

Federal Bureau of Investigation
Pennsylvania Avenue at 9th St. NW
Washington DC 20535

Resource List - Many resource lists exist for inmates. You should put together a list of all the resources you find during your incarceration. If you do not, there are many resources available through Transitional Service Centers. Normally, if you go to your local Social Services Office, they will have pamphlets and lists of resources for formerly incarcerated and those looking for housing, employment and other services. Many facilities carry pamphlets you can look at that have resource lists on them. The bottom line is that if you are sincere about getting the help that you need; you will always be able to find resources and organizations that are willing to help. If you are willing to put the work in, most are more than willing to help.

Résumé - Some states require that you attend a program in which you will create a résumé for yourself and a release plan before being released. If this is not the case in your state, you should have a professional-looking resume' put together to send to potential employers.

The Appendix has a section for Résumé Building and covers what a résumé should look like and what it should include.

Short/Long Term Goals - You should write out a list of short and long-term goals for yourself. This will provide something for you to work towards, and a sense of accomplishment when you set a long-term goal or obtain gainful employment within "one week" as a short-term goal. Do not set your aims too high, rather be realistic. If you are already living in a comfortable apartment, do not make one of your goals to "Own a house within six months." Be real about your goals. Eventually you will achieve them if you take your time and be patient. Remember, staying out of prison is the priority.

Social Security Card - You can get this through a Pre-releases Center or Transitional Services Center in your prison. You can also get it yourself by writing to the Social Security Administration address. Your prison counselor or Pre-release center will have that information for you. If you have never had a Social Security card, you should get one as soon as possible. Although prison will not let you have possession of the card itself, they will store it in your personal property until you are released.

Voter Registration - If you want to reinstate voting rights, as a citizen after parole and sentence is served, each state has different requirements. Some states will automatically restore your voting rights; other states such as Florida require additional paperwork from the courts and add costs for copying documents, registration etc. Research the state that you are in, and the state in which you may move to. Each state is different, and the state's regulations will be the ones followed. There is a federal mandate to restore your rights; individual states can and do make additional regulations. The paperwork needed to restore your voting rights is a court document clearly stating that you have completely served your incarceration time including parole; that you are now a free citizen. The system is terribly slow in recognizing this, so please make sure you have this paperwork from the courts, prison and/or parole officer. If you have no parole, get this before you leave prison. Register to VOTE. You cannot be heard without using your voice. Voting is one way to use your voice and be heard.

Time Management Plan - Let us face it, when you're released, you're going to find that you just don't have any time for the things you want to do! Create a time management plan for yourself. It could be something like this:

If you have a Job	*And if you do not*
8:00am – Go to Work	6:30am – Wake up
4:00pm – Go Home	7:00am – Breakfast
4:30pm – Dinner	7:30am – Job Search
5:30pm – Gym	12:00pm – Lunch
7:00pm – Home	12:30pm – Apt. Search
	5:00pm – Go home /

Job Search

Of course, these are examples, and your schedule will probably be different. But if you have a schedule, then you are much more organized and aware than someone who does not. Always be home on time if you have a curfew.

The Freedom of Information Act (FOIA): In the quest to obtain your necessary personal and vital documents, this law will make it easier to do so.

Every citizen of the United States can secure documentation from the Federal Government if they are a part and parcel of the public domain, unless it will be an invasion of another person's privacy.

In addition, most, if not all states, have a Federal counterpart to this Act commonly called the Freedom of Information Law (FOIL). In most cases, any documents that are public in nature are accessible to the public, except as mentioned above--if the information invades the privacy of another.

Therefore, almost all documents relating to you personally are accessible to you, unless exempt by a specific section of the law. To prepare oneself for successful transition into the community, it is recommended that documents you do not have (see preceding list on page 18 & 19) should be secured.

AFTER PRISON: A WAY TO SUCCEED

Listed below are documents that you will need to request from the Clerk of the Court in which you were convicted:

___Arrest Report(s)
___Commitment Papers
___Indictment(s)
___Judge's/District Attorney's statement(s)
___Plea Agreement(s)
___Sentencing/Trial Minutes

NOTES:

CHAPTER 3
Release Preparation

REMEMBER: ONE DAY AT A TIME.

***Here are most, if not all the things you should be acquiring or think about at least 6 months prior to release:

Six Months Preparation While Inside:

___Birth Certificate
___Credit Report
___Daily routine/habits
___Documents needed/Budget planning
___Driver's License/Unpaid Tickets
___Employment possibilities
___Funding Sources
___Housing possibilities
___Medical records/ Physical conditioning
___Miscellaneous paperwork if any

___Realistic goal planning
___Social Security Card/Benefits printout
___Time Management
___Warrants/ Certificates of Disposition / Rap
    Sheet

***These are some of the things you should work on for your first day out while you are still in prison.

First Day Release Preparation
While Inside:

___Appointments
___Bus ticket/Out of state transfer
___Cashing the release check
___Child Support
___Classified ads/ Job leads
___Access to the internet (libraries, job
    centers, etc.)
___Clothing
___Do you have a phone?
___Drug Counseling/ AA/ NA
___Entertainment
___Family visits

AFTER PRISON: A WAY TO SUCCEED

___First day expenses
___First day goals
___First day thoughts
___Identification
___Legal Issues
___Medical needs/ Medicaid card/ Medical Insurance
___Memo book/ Addresses / Phone Numbers / Contacts
___Metro card
___Parole clothes
___Picked up at facility?
___Place to live.
___PO name/ Interview/ Location/ Time/ Curfew
___Résumé package
___Spiritual Support/ Church/ Mosque/ Synagogue

***These are things you need to address somewhere around the second day after your release, after you have had a day or so to get reacquainted with being out of prison.

Second Day… Things to remember:

- Accountability for my whereabouts, times, etc.
- Breakfast/Lunch/Dinner
- Daily review – Accomplishments – Plan for tomorrow.
- Getting up and out – stay busy!
- Looking for employment – Filling out applications
- Recording my movements and places visited
- Where am I going? What am I doing today?

***Here are things you should try to accomplish during the first week you are released, a few days after you have become somewhat comfortable with being out of prison.

First Week Goals

- Apartment
- Continuing Medical needs/ HIV status

- Family matters
- Food
- Getting a group and sponsor – AA/NA or other
- Getting a job
- Having a rapport with your PO
- Laundry
- Memo book recording. *Save everything!*
- Relationships?
- Schooling
- Weekends – How will you handle them?

Remember, ***do not overwhelm yourself!*** These reminders and checkpoints are only here to tell you that these are the things you will have to be mindful of and go over before and after you are released. **Review them now!**

You have to make sure that you know about these things before you get out there because some people, especially those that have been locked up for a long time, don't know what they're getting into upon release. It is a changing world out there!

It is easy to have a daily schedule and have your life ruled by others while you are in jail. It is when you are released that you have to take charge and do all these things yourself. Few people and organizations will help you unless you are willing to help yourself.

You must make your own future!

Release Preparation

Think about these questions prior to your release date:

Where will you be staying?

Who will you be staying with?

Where will you be working?

41

What program(s) will you be attending?

Where is your nearest Parole Office?

When is your Parole reporting day?

Is all your paperwork in order? (check into it)

Do you have a valid ID? (If not get it)

Do you have transportation home? (If not get it)

> *If you do not have your documents or information that you will need that first day: get it or find out how to get it!!!!*

The Day of Release:
Things to Watch Out For:

Now here are some things you will need to watch out for:

People: Those who know you are getting released do not always have your best interests at heart. They may think it is time to "celebrate." You can easily go right back to your drug of choice or get drunk enough to do something that will send you right back to prison on the first day!

If you associated with people who were dealing drugs before you went to prison, they might think that now you're out, and that it's OK to be a part of that lifestyle again. That will just get you arrested again. Make new, better friends.

Place: If you must go back to the same neighborhood, you do not have to do the same things you were doing that got you arrested. If you live in a high-crime area, you will just have to be more diligent in staying away from the negativity.

Remember, going out to bars or nightclubs is normally a violation of your terms of parole!

Hanging out with a group of people on the street who are dealing or using drugs, even if you are not involved, can easily get you a violation or arrested!

If you have an Order of Protection against you do not go to the place that order designates. Not only will you violate parole if someone calls the police on you, but you will get a Contempt of Court charge for being there!

Things: There are many things you should be wary of on the day of release. You might have had a "stash" of drugs put somewhere when you got arrested that might still be there, or someone might be "holding" something for you. If you go to see your Parole Officer and they ask for a urine sample and you are dirty, you could have a violation even before you try to start off on the right foot!

If you used drugs, you might have para-phernalia lying around at home. If you do, have someone get rid of it before you get there! Or you might have guns or knives at home. Have them disposed of before you return to that environment! If you have a felony and are caught with a gun, it is an automatic violation and a new sentence nowadays. An exceptionally long one.

If the thing that brought you to prison was an argument with a certain person, and that person still lives in your building or neighborhood, you'll have to avoid them or try to get your parole address changed. A fight with them will bring you right back to prison, frequently with a violent assault charge accompanying it.

Even though alcohol is legal, in most cases, a term of your parole is: "I will not consume alcohol." If your Parole Officer smells alcohol on you, he or she can ask for a breathalyzer test. If you fail, it is a violation.

Sometimes the most innocent-seeming thing can get you violated. Being out of your house after curfew, possessing a knife or box cutter, driving a vehicle, or drinking a single beer or glass of wine are a few examples.

If your parole officer sees it or finds out about it, it can get you sent right back to prison.

CHAPTER 4
Parole Reporting

Parole reporting is the single most important issue you should concern yourself with. This is because, as you probably already know, parole has the authority to send you back to prison.

You must report to your local parole office at the earliest possible time after your release! And if you stop off at the local parole office even before stopping home and let them know that you did, you might even gain a small notch in the way of respect from our Parole Office.

Most of the time a person is sent back to prison on a violation because they did something wrong. It is not the PO's fault. Do not be one of the statistics; most Parole Officers have a difficult enough job without extra paperwork.

Do not give them a reason to violate you. If you are doing everything right and it seems as though your PO is picking on you ask to see a supervisor and explain the situation.

If you are doing wrong, well, then you will have to face the consequences of your actions sooner or later and don't blame your PO if he or she turns you in for violating your parole.

You must remember that the Division of Parole has seen and heard it all, so giving elaborate stories will not impress them in the least. It is the result they are looking for. If you are doing the right thing, your parole time will take care of itself and you will hardly even notice the passage of time.

Respect is the key when dealing with parole. Your Parole Officer is human, not an unsympathetic robot, and can be dealt with on human terms. If you are genuine with them and speak to them like a human, then they will treat you in kind. Any treatment contrary to this, especially if you are doing the right thing, should be reported to their supervisor in as calm a manner as possible.

Eventually, you may be considered inactive, at which time you may not have to report anymore and may only have to call once a week or month to let your Parole Officer know how you're doing.

Be able to account for your whereabouts at all times and make certain you comply with the conditions of your parole.

If you have a curfew, be home before the end of the curfew, and if you are not to frequent any establishments where alcohol is served, then stay away from them! It is common sense!

Do not contact any other parolees, as this is a cardinal rule of parole. If you see someone you once knew in prison, say your hellos and goodbyes and move on. If a parolee is a family member, make sure your Parole Officer knows this.

If you get a pass to go to another State on vacation, or to go on a vacation for several days or weeks, get it in writing from your PO. If you do not, you will not have any documented evidence that it was approved.

In fact, get everything in writing from your PO if you can. It may help you someday. If you are diligent about everything you do when you are out of your house (and sometimes in it), you will be successful in completing parole.

CHAPTER 5
An Example Release Program

Here is an example of a successful release program.

You should create your own at the end of this example. I suggest you use this as a template to guide you in the right direction. You do not have to do everything that is shown here. Just do what is relevant for you.

SHORT TERM

Week One
1) Report and establish a positive relationship with the PO
2) I am currently living with a family member
3) Go to the Department of Motor Vehicles (DMV). Request a non-driver's license identification card
4) Report to Social Services and apply for Medicaid and benefits
5) Establish with the PO an interview with an approved drug/ anti-violence program

6) Follow up on my next parole date. (Place it on calendar)

EMPLOYMENT

Week Two
1) Schedule with an organization an interview with Career Gear, to receive a voucher to get clothing for a job interview
2) Get copies of my résumé and cover letter
3) Go to the Department of Labor and request job search and employment assistance.
4) Request at the Department of Labor the W.O.T.C. form, which grants an employer a $3000 tax deduction for hiring me after 90 days. Also, the Federal Bonding Form, which insures me up to $5000 for the first year of employment
5) Get a job to hold me over until I can get one in my field
6) Attend outpatient daily or nightly AA/NA meetings
7) Follow up on my next parole date (Place it on calendar)

FINANCIAL PLAN

Week Three
1) I will go to the bank and open a savings account. Every payday I will deposit a minimum of $10 if possible.
2) I will also open a free checking account the same day, and use it to pay bills and transfer money into my savings account
3) I will begin to establish a line of credit by applying at Macy's for a credit card. I will also apply for a Capital One credit card. I will use them once a month for 6 months. I will pay the full balance to decrease them monthly interest rates
4) I will continue to attend outpatient daily or nightly AA/NA meetings
5) Follow up on my next parole date (Place it on calendar)

Week Four
1) Focus and reinforce all activities around my curfew
2) I get a small apartment with low rent

3) Notify my outpatient drug counselor of my interest in V.E.S.I.D (Vocational and Educational Services for Individuals With Disabilities)

4) Continue working and saving money

5) Attend outpatient daily or nightly AA/NA meetings

90 DAYS AFTER RELEASE

1) I am now eligible to apply for V.E.S.I.D technical training

2) Decide which career I want to pursue.

3) Decide to attend full or part-time training. It will depend on the school schedule and financial situation including how much money I have saved.

4) Continue attending outpatient daily or nightly AA/NA meetings

5) Follow up on my parole reporting date(s) and log them

6 MONTHS AFTER RELEASE

1) I will graduate from my 6-month outpatient drug program

2) I will keep my focus and study in my part-time vocational training

3) Continue to work part-time to pay my rent and bills

4) Request from your PO the opportunity to get a driver's license

5) Make sure if I request a change in curfew that I have valid reasons

6) Continue attending outpatient daily or nightly AA/NA meetings and self-help programs

7) Keep records of all my parole dates

1 YEAR AFTER RELEASE

1) Graduate from a college or vocational program

2) Continue to seek full-time employment of a career

3) A credit is established; I have buying power

4) Increase weekly savings deposits as my career builds

5) Continue attending outpatient daily or nightly AA/NA meetings and self-help programs

6) Log parole dates and request monthly reporting

LONG TERM GOALS

1) Continue attending outpatient daily or nightly AA/NA meetings and self-help programs

2) Begin dating the right partner

3) Start a family

4) Find a home and begin a new chapter with a partner I love and a family

---

A MAN OR WOMAN WITHOUT A PLAN IS ALREADY BEHIND IN LIFE. WITHOUT A PLAN OR GOALS, YOU CANNOT EXPECT TO SUCCEED.

This is the conclusion of the first five chapters. The author has given you many important aspects of how to succeed on parole when released and break the cycle of recidivism in the first five chapters. Without being honest with yourself, you might as well throw this book away or give it to someone who is willing to take the necessary steps to succeed.

A person who continues to do the same things hoping for a different result is misled and destined for failure. If you have been in prison before and what you did the last time did not work, try something different!

Admit to yourself that you are engaging in an insane pursuit that will only lead to you doing life in prison on the installment plan.

> **You should create a plan like the example on the previous pages. This will help you stay structured, and you will know what to do and where to go next without having to always remember!!**

INTERLUDE I
The Greatest and The Most

Here is a little break from the important stuff. If you always try to live by these ideals, you should be fine:

The most destructive habit   **WORRY**
The greatest joy   **GIVING**
The greatest loss   **LOSS OF SELF-RESPECT**

The most satisfying work
               HELPING OTHERS
The ugliest personality trait   **SELFISHNESS**
The most endangered species   **LEADERS**

Our greatest natural resource   **OUR YOUTH**
The Greatest "shot in the arm"
               ENCOURAGEMENT
The greatest problem to overcome   **FEAR**

The most effective sleeping pill
               PEACE OF MIND
The most crippling failure   **EXCUSES**
The most powerful force in life
               CREATIVITY

AFTER PRISON: A WAY TO SUCCEED

The most dangerous pariah	**A GOSSIP**
The World's most incredible computer	
	HUMAN BRAIN
The worst thing to be without	**HOPE**
The deadliest weapon	**THE TONGUE**
The two most powerful words	**"I CAN"**
The greatest asset	**FAITH**
The most worthless emotion	**SELF-PITY**
The most beautiful attire	**A SMILE**
The most prized possession	**INTEGRITY**

The most powerful channel of communication	
	PRAYER
The most contagious spirit	**ENTHUSIASM**

INTERLUDE II
Holding onto Positive Energy (HOPE)

Hope is the belief in something not yet realized, but nonetheless stimulates our consciousness. We, of course, hope that we will get out of prison, but that does not mean that we can do mothering to foster that hope. Hope, you see, is associated with action.

Hope, Like Energy, is Dynamic

The will to live is rooted in action. If we hope that tomorrow, we will be alive to accomplish something or anything, if it begins with our thoughts. How many times have we heard of people who have lost their hope to live when they were sick and not surprisingly, they die rather quickly?

On the other hand, there are those who are sick but have hope in living and many times get better simply due to that hope alone! This hope that we have is rooted in action (energy) of some unseen force. For many. It is a belief in a Creator or other benevolent Higher Power. Alcoholics Anonymous, and all other 12-step groups, dictate that we look to a Higher Power for hope in being sober or free from whatever addiction or habit that group addresses.

In many seemingly hopeless cases, it works.

How many of us have heard people say that they hope to be happy in life, and they believe that money will bring them happiness? There are many rich people who are unhappy; it is a known fact. It is not that happy people live life differently than unhappy people, but the fact is that happy people view life differently. They have a conscious hope that life will be happy in some way for them. It frequently is happy-- much more so than for those that do not believe in hope.

When I say that I hope to live to be a hundred, and then don't do anything to help make that hope a reality, I probably will have a lot less of a chance to live to that ripe old age. If a person is fooling themselves like this, they cannot really believe in the hope that they have unless they are just mouthing the words.

When people in prison say that they hope to no longer come back to jail after being released, and do nothing to prepare themselves for that hope, then they are simply speaking empty words that in all actuality carry no hope at all. They will most likely return to prison, floundering in their hopeless state.

The acronym **HOPE** stands for:
HOLDING ONTO POSITIVE ENERGY.

We can see the foundation of hope as not only something unseen, but also something you can help bring to life through positive action.

Home is where your heart is. Do not be fooled by the glitter of diamonds--even fake ones shine brightly! Depend on yourself. Emotions are poor masters but good servants. Do not allow your emotions to overrule your intelligence.

BEGINNING OF PART II

Now you can actively take part in your successful return to society, by filling in the blanks here in Part Two and putting down on paper your assets (for example, your education and employment). You can prepare that first day out and set yourself on the path to success. Without a good job, you will have difficulty "Living Well" and may resort back to crime to support yourself. Getting a good job that you enjoy will give you a great feeling of accomplishment, as well as allowing you to live well enough to enjoy life and purchase the things you like.

To get a good job, you'll need a good résumé, and this part of the book will help you with that and give you a few pointers on some more of the things you should watch out for that might land you back to prison.

> ### *Good Luck and Live Well!!*

CHAPTER 6
Preparing for the First Day

The Most Important One!

Now you can create your own personal profile and release plan using this book. This will help you get an idea of where you stand.

What are your objectives (plans) when released?

_____

_____

What are your employment possibilities when released?

_____

_____

List any Special Skills:

_____

_____

Family Status:
      ___Single ___Married ___Divorced

Number of children (if any): _____

Child Support Amount: $ _____

The following are reminders. Please check them off if they apply to you and if you have not obtained these, start getting them now!! You will need these things upon release:

Before release, are these documents in your file?

1. ___Birth Certificate
2. ___Social Security Card
3. ___Rap Sheet
4. ___Driver's Abstract
5. ___Medical records
6. ___Credit Report
7. ___Military papers
8. ___Resume

AFTER PRISON: A WAY TO SUCCEED

Before release, have you obtained?

1. ___Letter(s) of assurance of employment
2. ___A place to stay
3. ___Programs to attend (List Programs Below)
4. ___Address of Parole Officer
5.___ Suitable Clothing

THE DAY OF RELEASE

Here are the things you will need to be concerned with on the day you are released:

1) Where will you be staying?

_____

2) Who will you be staying with?

_____

3) Where will you be working?

_____

4) What program(s) will you be attending?

_____

5) Where is your nearest Parole Office?

_____

6) When is your Parole reporting day?

_____

7) Is all your paperwork in order? [ ]Y or [ ]N
If not, what else do you need?

8) Do you have a valid ID? [ ]Y or[ ]N
If not, how and when will you get it?

_____

9) Do you have transportation home?
[ ]Y or [ ]N *If not,* name potential people or
ways you can get home:

_____

> ***If you do not have your
> documents or information that
> you will need that first day: get it
> or find out how to get it!!!!***

CHAPTER 7
Finances & Living Well

Problems with money and the inability to budget income efficiently can be some of the minor factors a person who is trying to do the right thing might turn back to crime.

These are things you will have to be aware of that you will be paying for when you get on your feet and start making money. Fill in those that apply to you:

MONTHLY REGULAR EXPENSE AMOUNTS:

CHILD CARE/ SUPPORT: $_____

GROCERIES/ FOOD: $_____

HEALTH CARE:

    Medications: $_____

    Eye Care/ Glasses: $_____

    Dental: $_____

INSURANCE:

    Car: $_____

    Medical: $_____

    Life: $_____

Home/ Rental: $_____
INTERNET COSTS (Necessity):$ _____
RENT/ MORTGAGE: $_____
BOARDING: $_____
TAXES:
    Income: $_____
    House: $_____
TELEPHONE: $_____
CELL PHONE: $_____
*TELEVISION/ CABLE / INTERNET (often
these are bundled together with a contract):
                                          $_____
TRANSPORTATION: $_____
OTHER: $_____
OTHER: $_____
OTHER: $_____

TOTAL MONTHLY REGULAR EXPENSES:

$ _____

MONTHLY INFREQUENT EXPENSES
AMOUNTS

Books Magazines/Reading Material: $_____
Clothing/ Footwear: $_____
Cosmetics/ Hygiene/ Personal Care: $_____
Credit Card Payments: $_____
Entertainment/ Movies/ Etc.: $_____
Gifts: $_____
Home Cleaning Supplies: $_____
Home Maintenance: $_____
Pet Food/ Supplies: $_____
Restaurants: $_____
Vacation: $_____
Vehicle Expenses/ Repairs/ Gas/ Tolls:
                              $_____

TOTAL MONTHLY INFREQUENT EXPENSES:

$ _____

CHAPTER 8
Some Words on Employment

This is one of the most difficult issues among those being released from prison. Frequently, a person is released having obtained a college degree or some important training while incarcerated and finds that it is nearly impossible to find a job only because of his or her prior criminal record. It is an even sadder situation for someone who was once in a productive job situation and became involved with drugs, which usually leads to crime, and when released--find that he or she has extreme difficulty obtaining employment in their specific field.

You will need to put together a good résumé and determine how to handle the job application, especially the part where it says, "Have you ever been convicted of a crime?"

A usable résumé will allow you to better understand what you have to offer and will be used by you in approaching employment opportunities. DO NOT pad your résumé. Be truthful. It will be the fastest way to lose the employment opportunity if someone asks you about what information you have given. Remember: the technology today can reveal the padding/ oversight within seconds of an employer's inquiry. Most employers hire a contracting company to verify the backgrounds of all potential employees; even before the interview is completed.

Honesty is the Best Policy

Honesty is the best policy in this respect. With the onset of the terrorist attacks of 9/11/2001, a number of "services" have sprung up, (profitable ones of course), that make it very easy for a potential employer to look up a specific person and see if he or she has ever been convicted of a crime. It could have been the most harmless crime, and if it shows up (and it will!), there is a good chance you will not be hired. This makes it extremely difficult for a person released from prison, who has a conviction to be successful by getting a job and being productive in order to help prevent a return to prison.

The Appendix includes a sample application, cover letter and résumé.

Remember that the format and information will change as the job markets change. The included sample application is for your records and is a good worksheet to keep your information handy. Carry this with you to places of employment who will give you their paper application to fill out. Please note that most of_all applications will be completed online using computers (including state benefits, healthcare registration, etc.). They are tedious and taxing on patience. Be patient.

Yes, you do need computer skills to apply for most jobs / benefits. You also need an email account and address. Public libraries have free classes to learn the basics including keyboarding and typing (you need these to use a computer effectively). Employment centers and libraries have free computer time. Get a library card to access all this free information and great resources.

Résumé's and cover letters need to have the words describing the job you are applying for included.   For example, if the skill of "carpenter" is listed in the job advertisement, then make sure those exact words are in your résumé and cover letter, so that if you are searching for a job as a carpenter on the computer and your résumé states that you worked at "Mastercraft Woodworking" as a carpenter from 2010-2015, your skills will match the hiring managers' requirements, and you have a better chance of getting the job. Essentially, the computer is looking for "key words" from your résumé to match the job description and skill set needed for the job. Use your online resources to review/download/use current formats for resumes and cover letters. You do not have to pay for this service. It is online. It is free.

Keep up with the latest using YOUR resources from Career Source Centers, Employment Offices, and Libraries.

If you answered "yes" to "Have you ever been convicted of a felony?" I recommend you do; you will no doubt have to explain this. I recommend that you be as honest as you can do not glorify the crime. _Never say_ you "made a mistake" just admit guilt (if you were guilty) and remind your potential employer that you have come to terms with this and have moved on. Remind him or her that you can be federally bonded, and that your potential employer will get a hefty tax break for you. There are millions of people working out there that have crime under their belt; it's not the stigma it is sometimes made out to be. You CAN get a job, usually an incredibly good one, if you have done your time. Be persistent and have faith.

If you have saved some money while incarcerated or have family or others out there to back you, think of starting your OWN business. (Know that you will have to OK it with your PO to own your own business).

There are many businesses out there that hire ONLY those released from prisons and I'm happy to say, many of them have less problems than some businesses that stubbornly choose to hire those that have never been to prison.

You can make your prison time a time of learning and reflection, or you can make it a time that is wasted and non-productive. We all have choices, no matter how small--even in prison. Start making good choices NOW!

References

You should have already written them down, so you do not need them here, where they will be provided to a potential employer, upon request. Make sure they are available to provide once the request is given.

That is all there is to it! If you make it look professional. I suggest using a computer with the Microsoft Word program and a good printer with résumé paper. If you have the right skills for the job you are trying to get, you will have a good chance to get the kind of job you're looking for.

If you explain everything honestly and convey to an employer your sincere desire to remain out of prison and stay clean and clear from crime, YOU WILL BE SUCCESSFUL

Some more things to remember are:

If you get a call from your prospective employer to appear for an interview: dress appropriately for the type of job you are applying for. If it is an office job, a suit and tie are usually required, and if it's a manual labor job of some type: you should wear pressed pants (or jeans) and a clean, pressed shirt.

If you are nervous, try not to let your potential employer know it! Get to the point, and try to conduct yourself in a respectful, calm manner. If you have to explain your criminal record, do so without getting into too many details and let your potential employer know you're bettering yourself in every way possible and have moved beyond whatever it was that brought you to prison.

If you are hired, let him or her know that your PO may stop by occasionally to check upon you. Again, if you are honest and your demeanor reflects it, you will soon end up right where you want to be.

The reality is that you may end up putting in a hundred applications and all your college and experience means nothing when you say you have a felony. What do you do?

As a rule: the PO will not get on you for a couple of months but after that they will be on you like white on rice. If you cannot find a job, think about volunteering somewhere. You would be amazed at the contacts that can be made when you volunteer.

Also, most states have some type of JOB link that offers free help in writing resumes, making copies, job listings, job hunting classes and computer classes, etc. If all else fails, think about the possibilities of starting your own business.

If you have not practiced keeping a good filing system, then you must begin to practice before you get out. Filing all your movements, conditions, purchases, job applications, etc. is especially important. If you cannot afford a filing cabinet get some good sturdy boxes and tall folders to which each item can be marked.

Having a filing system will also give your life more order – an important Aspect of being successful on parole and *IN LIFE!*

Make a list of skills/ hobbies below that might interest a potential employer.

CHAPTER 9
Parole Conditions

Whatever your conditions, make sure you understand what they mean. If you have a new PO, ask them to go over the conditions with you and ask them to initialize the bottom after you do. If they cannot give you an answer concerning the conditions that have been placed upon you – circle that condition and ask to speak with a supervisor.

If the PO changes your conditions or modifies your curfew, make sure it is in writing and you have a copy.

Expect a different PO at the slightest change; and remember what you had may not be what you get. That is the way it goes sometimes.

Be respectful always. You will earn the PO'S' trust and then you may be switched again. Mention to the new PO the positive relationship you had with your last PO. Tell him or her that you want to do the right thing. If you cannot get along with the PO, ask to speak with a supervisor but the best advice is to take the time to get to know your PO and do what they tell you.

Well, you have finally been released and given your state money in many cases and the money that you have saved in a check form.

Make sure that before you leave that you have all your personal property, your state ID, Parole Papers, and any other personal items you plan to take with you.

If you have medication to take, make sure you take it before you walk out the door. Many state facilities will search your property on the way out, so do not be foolish. If you have something in your property that you are not supposed to have, you could be violated before you walk out the door.

If you have someone coming to pick you up, be prepared to leave the prison premises immediately. Do not take any pictures or do anything stupid. Again, you could be charged with a crime before you leave state property, and you will be back inside before you can blink your eyes.

AFTER PRISON: A WAY TO SUCCEED

RESOURCE LIST:

_____

_____

_____

_____

IMPORTANT PHONE NUMBERS:

_____

_____

_____

_____

CHAPTER 10
HOME SWEET HOME

How many of us have said--throughout the time we served--that we cannot wait until we get home. Yet if you look at the statistics, you will see that 75% of the men released will be back inside within three years. How can this happen? Many men forget the rough times. Men have told me that they forgot until the handcuffs were put on; then everything came back to them. So how do we break the cycle?

One of the most important aspects of returning home is to have a support system and enough MONEY to survive. If that means saving $1.00 a week for the next ten years while you do a stretch or every time you are sent some money from outside make sure you either send it to someone you can trust at home or disciple yourself and do not spend it in the commissary. I know how hard that is. I have been there, but if you want to raise your chances of success you must start saving now.

Sure, we all get the $40.00 of our own money upon release but that will not last one day. Everything is expensive. If you have a good paying prison job, then start saving. If you do not have a good paying prison job, then save what you make and pray for a better job. It will come. Be patient.

Write letters to family, friends, and anybody else who will listen and assist and try and start saving your nest egg. Having some savings can be the difference between success and failure when you first get out.

If your family sends you packages on a regular basis, ask them to save a portion of the money for you. Another way to save is to "force save." When you see something that you like in a magazine or on TV, instead of buying what you do not need--order a gold ring and have it sent home. You can always cash it in later. Even better would be to have a close, trusting relative buy savings bonds. As you do your time, the bonds will mature and when you are released you will have the funds you need to get an apartment, eat, etc. Start thinking smarter.

We have all heard that money is the root of all evil. When you have money upon your

81

release, you will not be tempted to do something stupid to survive and wind up back in prison for it. That is what makes the difference.

In addition, although many of us have become educated while in prison or learned different trades, do not expect the business world to open its arms to you. Insurance companies fear those who have been formerly incarcerated. I have had employers tell me that they would like to hire me, but the insurance company will never go for it.

The first day or week out you should have no idea about finding your career employment. Find work no matter what it is; and if you cannot find work, then find some place that will let you volunteer. My first job was as a volunteer feeding the hungry. Eventually I was able to land a part-time job and later was offered a full-time position. **Smart steps are slow steps sometimes.**

When you first get out, many states have no help for you at all. In Florida, nobody gets medical coverage and your Picture ID from the prison system cannot be used as a valid ID to get a driver's license or state ID. You must have a social security card, birth certificate and your release papers. If you have been incarcerated for a long time, ever since 9/11 things have changed. If you have a driver's license, try and renew it while you are inside. This will save a lot of aggravation and money when you are out.

In many states, there is no public transportation. Contact someone you know and ask them to keep an eye out for a used bicycle. I rode a bike the first three months after release. If you are lucky enough to have a relative or family member that drives, they can help you out too. If all else fails, walk.

Any way that you can get your life back in order is the best way. Besides, riding a bike keeps you in shape, and with the price of gas getting higher, it will help you save more money and get further ahead.

If you can get a car, make sure that you have a proper registration, plates and insurance. The technological age only takes an onboard computer in every police car seconds to find out if you are driving legally or not. Do not be stupid. Police contact must be reported to your

PO even if it was only for a traffic violation. Who needs the hassle!

A TYPICAL FIRST DAY OUT

- See my parents, wife, children, etc.
- Have a good meal.
- Pray.
- Unpack and get settled.
- Take a long bath or shower.
- Watch a good movie or television show.
- Use a cell phone to make a call.
- Make plans for tomorrow.
- Be comfortable.
- Remember some of the things I once missed.
- Take a deep breath of clean, crisp, free air!
- Go to sleep in my own bed.
- Dream of a good future.
- Awaken the next day refreshed and a free person!

- Do not get discouraged if everything does not work out the way I want it to.

REMEMBER:

EVEN THOUGH YOU HAVE LEARNED MANY THINGS DURING YOUR INCARCERATION, IT MUST INCLUDE WHAT YOU HAVE LEARNED ABOUT YOURSELF. ASK YOURSELF AND REFLECT ON THESE QUESTIONS:

WHY DID I MAKE THE MISTAKES THAT BROUGHT ME HERE IN THE FIRST PLACE?

WHAT AM I GOING TO DO DIFFERENTLY WHEN I AM RELEASED?

CHAPTER 11
Conclusion

Remember, sometimes the slightest thing, something you might do every day had you not been on parole, has the capacity to get you violated. With the recidivism rate bolstered by a plague of non-criminal parole violations why be a part of it?

If you have a solid enthusiasm in your mind to stay out of prison, you can do it, as long as you always remember where you are, what you're doing and who you're doing it with. Some formerly incarcerated individuals believe it is far easier to go back to prison than to stay out. Do not kid yourself, this author has done twenty years in prison, begs to differ.

Wasn't it difficult to plan and plot a particular crime, or to look for drugs and buy them? Would not it have just been easier to look for a job or avoid whatever situation it was that led you to do that crime? If you really look at the situation, it is always easier to remain a law-abiding citizen and stay away from the voracious prison system, which will always be there waiting for you to return if you allow it.

> **Take control of the rest of your life NOW*!!*

> ***I know that if I keep trying to stay on the right path, step by step I will get to where I need to be.***

Note:
Remember to take precautions against the Coronavirus Pandemic currently sweeping the Globe in this year, 2020, and 2021.

Please feel free to share your reflections with me. I would love to hear from you! Your thoughts can serve as encouragement and a guide for someone who thinks all hope is lost.

You can reach me by email at:

John@prison-reentry.com
www.prison-reentry.com

*If you enjoyed this book and find it
useful, please take a few moments to
write a review on your favorite store, and
please refer it to anyone you know that
may benefit from the information inside.*

APPENDIX
Resume & Cover Letter

Cover Letter

Wondering what to include in your cover letter? It is a good idea to include key points about why you are a great fit for the company and the best choice for the specific job. Of course, do not forget to ask for the interview—but keep it brief!

A cover letter should not read like a novel, no matter how great a plot you have. Remember to THANK the person for reviewing your qualifications and FOLLOW-UP with a thank you note, or e-mail once interviewed. (If you do not hear anything, follow-up in two days, if no response, move on. Companies are not letting the candidates know unless they are directly interviewing)

[Your Name]
[Street Address] | [City, ST ZIP Code] | [Phone] | [Email] (must have for contact by employer)
[Date]
 [Title]
[Company]
[Address]
[City, ST ZIP Code]

Attn: _____

AFTER PRISON: A WAY TO SUCCEED

Re: Job Position Title and reference #/ Job ID # (if applicable)

Dear [Recipient (use attn. line for name] or Human Resources Manager or Department Manager:

Sincerely,

[Your Name] (Remember to sign if submitting this to a person or directly to company in paper format if not, print your name with computer as signature).

Resume

Your address
Phone #
E-mail address

[Your Name]
[Street Address] | [City, ST ZIP Code] | [phone] | [email]
(must have e-mail to be contacted)

Skills (use this area to match the skills in the advertisement for the job) – remember to update resume for EACH job application – make sure to use the words in the advertisement for each job you are applying to – yes, a new resume & cover letter for EVERY job you want.
[To replace tip text with your own, just select a line of text and start typing. For best results when selecting text to copy or replace, do not include space to the right of the characters in your selection.]

AFTER PRISON: A WAY TO SUCCEED

Experience
[Dates From] – [To]
[Job Title] | [Company Name] | [Location]
[This is the place for a brief summary of your key
responsibilities and most stellar accomplishments.] –
Use the key words in the job description to match the
most relevant skills per position]

Education (if no education, delete this section and do not
mention unless asked in interview or is a requirement
listed in job advertisement).
[School Name, City, State] (Even if GED or a specific
grade level).
 [Major] (If no major, then do not include).
Certificates of Vocational Education (name of certificate,
issuing institution – may need explanation of skills used
during certifying process if confusing).
Certificates of Completion (name and institution).
Do not include your GPA// Do not include your
graduation date.

Volunteer Experience (additional skills not noted above
– computer software/hardware or repair of something
skills providing Added Value for Employer).

Outline this area with dates and time and contacts for the
organizations you have volunteered for or provided
services to -- use experience section to guide the
formatting.

Job Application Form Sample:

AFTER PRISON: A WAY TO SUCCEED

***Use this as a guide – most applications are online only & you will need ALL this information to complete applications – be prepared to have 10 years employment history available – just in case).

Instructions: Print clearly in black or blue ink. Answer all questions. Sign and date the form.

Personal Information

First Name_____

Middle Name_____

Last Name_____

Street Address_____

City, State, Zip Code_____

Phone Number (___) _____

Email_____

Have you ever applied to / worked for Company before?
[] Y or [ ] N

If yes, please explain (include date):

_____
_____

Do you have any friends, relatives, or acquaintances working for Company?
[ ] Y or [ ] N

If yes, state name & relationship:

_____

AFTER PRISON: A WAY TO SUCCEED

If hired, would you have transportation to/from work? [ ] Y or [ ] N

Are you over the age of 18? [ ] Y or [ ] N

If you are under age 18, do you have an employment/age certificate? [ ] Y or [ ] N

If hired, would you be able to present evidence of your U.S. citizenship or proof of your legal right to work in the United States? [ ] Y or [ ] N

Have you been convicted of or pleaded no contest to a felony within the last five years?
[ ] Y or [ ] N

If yes, please describe the crime - state nature of the crime(s), when and where convicted and disposition of the case.

If hired, are you willing to submit to and pass a controlled substance test? [ ] Y or [ ] N

Position and Availability:
Position Applied For: _____

Salary desired: $_____

Are you applying for:

AFTER PRISON: A WAY TO SUCCEED

Temporary work – such as summer or holiday work? [ ]
Y or [ ] N
Regular part-time work? [ ] Y or [ ] N
Regular full-time work? [ ] Y or [ ] N
Days/Hours Available
Monday _____
Tuesday _____
Wednesday _____
Thursday _____
Friday _____
Saturday _____
Sunday _____

Hours Available: from _____ to _____
If applying for temporary work, when will you be
available? _____

If hired, on what date can you start working?
____ / ____ / ____

Can you work on the weekends? [ ] Y or [ ] N

Can you work evenings? [] Y or [ ] N

Are you available to work overtime?
[ ] Y or [ ] N

Are you able to perform the essential functions of the job
for which you are applying, with / without reasonable
accommodation?
[ ] Y or [ ] N

AFTER PRISON: A WAY TO SUCCEED

If no, describe the functions that cannot be performed.

_____

Education, Training and Experience
High School

School name: _____

School address:

_____
School city, state, zip:

_____
_____
Number of years completed: _____
Did you graduate? [ ] Y or [ ] N
Degree / diploma earned: _____

College / University:
School name: _____
School address:_____
School city, state, zip:

_____
_____
Number of years completed: _____
Did you graduate? [ ] Y or [ ] N
Degree / diploma earned: _____
Vocational School:
School Name: _____
Address:_____
School city, state, zip:

AFTER PRISON: A WAY TO SUCCEED

_____
_____
Number of years completed: _____
Did you graduate? [ ] Y or [ ] N
Degree / diploma earned:_____

Military:
Branch: _____
Rank in Military:_____
Total Years of Service: _____
Skills/duties: _____
Related details:_____
Skills and Qualifications: Licenses, Skills, Training,
Awards

_____

Do you speak, write or understand any foreign
languages? [ ] Y or [ ] N
If yes, describe which languages(s) and how fluent of a
speaker you consider yourself to be.

_____

Employment History
You should be prepared to detail each position for the
past five (possibly 10) years, and **account for any gaps**
in employment during that period.
Are you currently employed? [ ] Y or [ ] N
If you are currently employed, may we contact your
current employer? [ ] Y or [ ] N
Name of Employer: _____
Name of Supervisor: _____

AFTER PRISON: A WAY TO SUCCEED

Telephone Number: _____

Business Type: _____

Address: _____

City, state, zip: _____

Length of Employment (Include Dates):

_____

Position & Duties: _____

Reason for Leaving:

_____

Previous Positions:

Include for each employer/position for the past five years:

Name of Employer: _____

Name of Supervisor: _____

Telephone

Number:_____

Business Type: _____

Address:_____

City, state,

zip:_____

Length of Employment (Include Dates):

_____

Position & Duties:_____

Reason for Leaving:

_____

May we contact this employer for references?

[ ] Y or [ ] N

References

AFTER PRISON: A WAY TO SUCCEED

List below three persons who have knowledge of your work performance within the last four years. Please include professional references only.

HINT: most employers will use this method for the fastest response time – let your references know about each time you use his/her name reference with the employer name, position title and who will contact him/her – get permission from them FIRST! You do not want a bad reference – employers talk to one another especially day jobs and recruiters for temp agencies, restaurants, machine shops etc.

Name - First, Last:

_____

Telephone Number:_____
Address:_____
City, State, Zip: _____

Occupation:_____
Number of Years Acquainted:_____
E-mail Address:_____
Name - First, Last:

_____

Telephone Number:_____
Address:_____
City, State, Zip:_____
Occupation:_____
Number of Years Acquainted:_____
Name - First, Last:

_____

AFTER PRISON: A WAY TO SUCCEED

E-mail Address:_____

Telephone Number:_____

Address:_____

City, State, Zip:_____

Occupation: _____

Number of Years Acquainted: _____

I certify that information contained in this application is true and complete. I understand that false information may be grounds for not hiring me or for immediate termination of employment at any point in the future if I am hired. I authorize the verification of any or all information listed above.

Signature_____

Date_____

NOTES:

JOURNAL:

JOURNAL

AFTER PRISON: A WAY TO SUCCEED

JOURNAL

103

Made in the USA
Las Vegas, NV
05 March 2025

19082987R00059